THE **Nile**

LIFELINE OF EGYPT

NILE

Lifeline of Egypt

by Violet Weingarten

Illustrations by Ronni Solbert
Maps by Fred Kliem

GARRARD PUBLISHING COMPANY
CHAMPAIGN, ILLINOIS

Sailboats on the Nile
at Cairo.
Ewing Galloway

Nancy Larrick, Ed.D.
is the Educational Advisor for this Series.

The Nile at Aswan.

Egyptian State Tourist Administration

Contents

The Great Sphinx

1. A River of Contrasts

The Nile is a river of contrasts.

Imagine the river, and you see Egyptians—distant, mysterious, proud. You think of pyramids and the Great Sphinx, staring across the endless desert. These monuments were erected beside the Nile over 4,000 years ago. They were ancient when Cleopatra, the last queen of old Egypt, sailed down the river on her gilded barge.

History was made along the Nile. Men have lived and kept records in its valley for over 60 centuries. The Egyptians developed geometry, arithmetic and astronomy there. They invented a calendar so that they could keep track of the river's ebb and flow. Some of the greatest works of art the world has ever known were produced on the banks of the Nile. Some of the most remarkable structures on earth still stand there.

The Bible is full of stories about the Nile. It was the river on which a pharaoh's daughter discovered the baby Moses floating in a rush basket. Here the people of Israel worked as slaves, helping to build the pyramids. And here Joseph won the king's favor by storing grain from fields along the Nile for the times when crops were scarce.

Today more than twenty-six million Egyptians depend on the river for food, water, electric power and transportation.

But the Nile is more than an Egyptian river. Before it enters Egypt it has been on its way for over 3,000 miles. It has passed through Central Africa, Ethiopia and the Sudan.

The Nile is the longest river in Africa and the second longest in the world. It rises in snow-

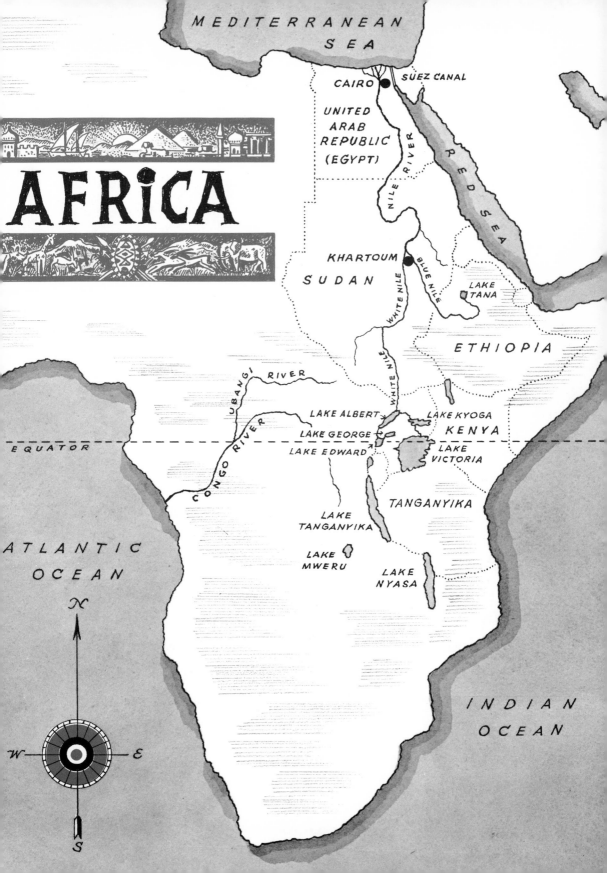

capped mountains and flows through steaming jungles. In Egypt, the Nile Valley is surrounded by the biggest desert on earth. Farther south, the river flows through huge lakes and over nearly a dozen waterfalls. It is navigable for 2,900 miles. This is almost as far as from New York to San Francisco.

The Nile was one of the first rivers to be used by man, but parts of it are still unknown. Its source was located less than a hundred years ago. Explorers still make expeditions up the Nile. Archaeologists still find rare treasures along its sandy banks.

Even if you knew nothing about its history or geography, the Nile would still be interesting. It has so many animals—hippopotamuses, elephants, antelopes, rhinoceroses and the like—that a great wildlife reservation has been established at Murchison Falls near one of its sources. Thousands of African and European birds migrate along the river. In the fall, its banks are so jammed with birds that often they must wait their turn to land, like airplanes over a crowded airport.

And if that isn't enough, the Nile these days is a wonderful spot for people interested in construction. For across the river at Aswan, the United Arab Republic is building the biggest dam in the world.

Hippos sun and swim in the Nile.

2. North to the Mediterranean

Nearly 3,500 years ago, an Egyptian king, or pharaoh, called Thutmose led his army as far as the Euphrates River in Syria. It was the first large river other than the Nile that he had ever seen. When he described it later, he did not bother to name it. He simply called it the "Water That Flows the Wrong Way."

As far as the Egyptians were concerned, there was only one right way for a river to go. That was the way the Nile flowed. Looking at a map, we might think this peculiar. Unlike most rivers, the Nile flows from south to north. To go south along the Nile is to go up, and to go north is to go down. It is the only river which rises near the equator and flows into the temperate zone. From its most remote source, the Nile is the second longest river on earth. If it were put in the Western Hemisphere, the Nile would reach from Central America across the United States into Canada.

Actually, the Nile is two rivers. One starts in Central Africa, where it is known as the White Nile. The White Nile's source is over 4,000 miles from its outlet at the Mediterranean Sea. Halfway along its journey to the sea, the White Nile meets the Blue Nile, which rises in a sacred spring in the mountains of Ethiopia. The two rivers join near Khartoum in the Sudan. Thereafter, they flow as one river. The Nile has one more tributary, the Atbara. Then for 1,600 miles, it flows through rainless deserts to the sea.

To this day, it is impossible to navigate parts of the Nile. But if you follow the river by plane, you see almost every variety of landscape imaginable.

The White Nile starts by draining four lakes, named Edward, Albert, George and Victoria. If the names seem a bit strange for Central Africa, there is a simple explanation. The explorers who discovered them were English, and they named them after members of the British royal family.

Lake Albert and Lake Edward are on the equator, surrounded by hot, humid jungles. Between them are mountains so high that their tops are covered with snow the year around. This whiteness so bewildered the natives who had never seen snow that they named the mountains *Ruwenzori*, meaning *Mountains of the Moon*. They thought that the mountains had caught the moonlight. George is a small lake; Victoria is much larger.

One side of Lake Victoria has many banana plantations. The area is full of butterflies. At

14

By Burton Holmes from Ewing Galloway

The Mountains of the Moon, usually hidden by clouds, are rarely visible for more than ten minutes at a time. February is the best time to view them. The highest peaks, which are 17,000 feet, are always covered with snow.

certain seasons of the year, there are crashing thunderstorms every day. Hippopotamuses and crocodiles sun themselves at Ripon Falls, where the White Nile leaves the lake. The birds crossing Africa gather in quiet marshes nearby. The air is filled with their flashing wings—gold, silver, purple, red and blue. There are cranes, finches,

15

Storks enjoy the quiet waters of Lake Edward. Sabena World Airlines

ibises, kingfishers, herons, nightingales, egrets, storks and starlings.

On the other side of Lake Victoria, there is a modern port with freshly painted steamers at the piers. Jet planes roar into the airfield nearby.

After the Nile leaves Lake Victoria, it is a quiet stream for a while. Then it squeezes itself through a narrow cleft. It drops 120 feet in a roaring waterfall—Murchison Falls—before it is gentle again. The jungle comes right to the bank, which is overgrown with bushes and vines. The only path is the river itself.

Antelopes and zebras drink from its blue-green waters. Monkeys chatter, birds call, frogs croak, and there is the steady hum of insects.

Suddenly, after miles of peaceful drifting, the river seems to choke from floating masses of grass and trees, called *sudd*. Mile after mile of swamp closes in. It seems as if nothing could ever get through. Here and there, a block of matted vegetation breaks off, and a small muddy channel appears. The growth is so thick that it can support an elephant. Occasionally, you can see one standing on a moving island of vegetation.

The sudd is so thick an elephant can stand on it.

P.I.P. photo by PRESSEHUSET

The Nile provides a living for many fishermen. The decorative nets are thrown and hauled in hundreds of times a day.

The sudd region extends for 475 miles. In the wet season, it covers an area as big as England.

The sudd soaks up the Nile like a sponge. It is made up of papyrus reeds, razor-sharp sword grass, elephant grass, bamboo and the thorny ambatch tree. Blue water hyacinths and purple lotuses cover it.

Years ago, steamers tore channels in the sudd to get through. Now the sudd is burned off. Chunks are cut with huge saws and towed away, leaving a channel 40 or 50 yards wide. Paddle steamers going through the sudd are careful to

18

cover their decks with wire netting, for the mosquitoes are vicious.

The Blue Nile starts in Ethiopia, 9,000 feet above sea level, in a spring near Lake Tana. This is a region of wild summer storms. Sometimes there may be 400 thunderstorms in a single season, with hailstones so big they kill men and cattle.

After the river leaves Lake Tana, it reaches Tisisat Falls, one of the world's wildest and biggest falls. Tisisat means *roaring fire*. The falls

Channels are cut through the sudd to allow boats' passage.

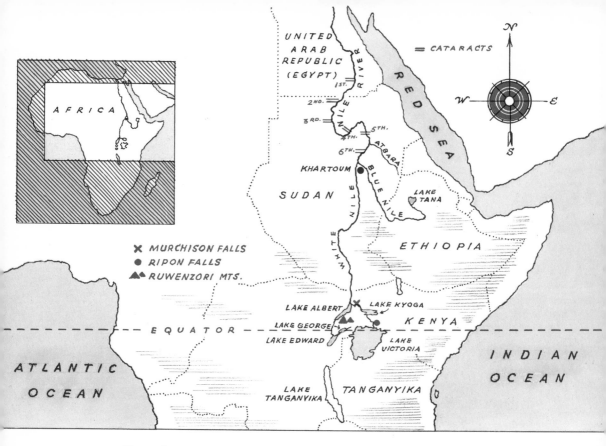

really do seem on fire because of the reddish rainbow in their heavy spray. After the falls, the river drops into a mile-deep gorge. The water churns, even in the dry season, until it reaches the Sudan. During the rainy season, the Blue Nile is a torrent. Some of its water is now held back by the Sennar Dam, in the central Sudan. But the Blue Nile still supplies three-fourths of the water of the Nile proper.

Soon after the Blue Nile and the White Nile

meet, the combined river begins its descent into Egypt. It does so by a series of waterfalls, or cataracts, which act as giant steps. There are six of these. From ancient times, they have been numbered as if one were going downstairs into Egypt from the Sudan. The Sixth Cataract is just north of Khartoum. The First Cataract, which is the most famous, is at Aswan. Once, the First Cataract marked the limits of Egypt. At this point there is an island called Elephantine. It got this name because it was once the entrance to Ethiopia, which the ancient Egyptians called the Land of Elephants.

From Khartoum on, the Nile is an Egyptian river.

When the river floods, it leaves rich earth behind.

3. Where Flood Means Food

Without the Nile, there would be no Egypt. The whole land would be desert. In one year Egypt has no more rain than might fall in Ohio on a single summer's day. People, crops and animals are almost completely dependent on the river for their water supply.

But the Nile does more than provide water for Egypt. It is responsible for its fertile black soil.

Every summer, just when you would expect a river flowing through hot rainless deserts to dry up, the Nile rises. By autumn, it is so high that it overflows its banks, drenching the land. In December, the river returns to normal. But as it does, it leaves behind a rich deposit of earth, or silt. This earth is so fertile that it yields two or three crops a year, if properly watered.

The first Egyptians did not know how the Nile could do this each year. Today we know that one of its sources is in the mountains of Ethiopia. Heavy summer rains turn the Blue Nile into a torrent. It flows down the hillsides with such force that it scrapes off the topsoil. This mass of water and soil rushes on to meet the White Nile. The combined stream carries tons of soil thousands of miles into Egypt, now known as the United Arab Republic.

Over the years, the river has built up a rich valley varying in width from a few yards to 15 or 20 miles at the most. Near its mouth, it has made a wide fertile area called the *delta*, because it has the triangular shape of the fourth letter of the Greek alphabet. The Nile Valley and its delta comprise only three per cent of Egypt's land today. But 95 per cent of the population lives there. This is practically the only fertile area in the country.

Life in ancient Egypt was controlled by the Nile. The land it had brought down from Ethiopia made up the entire land of the kingdom. The early Egyptians built their villages on the outer edge of the river valley, so they would not cover good soil with houses. They called their country "The Two Banks." Their definition of an Egyptian was "any man who drinks from the Nile." Since the Nile flows north, their word for north was *downstream*, as their word for south was *upstream*.

Hunger or plenty depended on the Nile. The river always flooded, but some years it rose too little and other years it rose too much. If the river rose less than 20 feet, it did not water enough land and crops were scarce. If it rose 30 feet or more, it swept away houses and fields. So

*A shaduf, from an
1877 engraving.*

the Egyptians had to learn how to control floods and store water for use when the river was low again.

It was too big a job for one man. All had to work together. Some made catch basins and dams. Others caught water in skins or pots of Nile clay and carried it to plots beyond the river. Egyptian peasants still use the *shaduf*. This is an arrangement of a bucket and a pole, by which one man can lift a good deal of water from the river in the course of a day.

This small boy spends his day prodding the camel around a circle to turn a water wheel.

At first, the people of a village worked together. Then its people united with other villages in order to control the river along more of its course. In time, governments were formed to direct work on the river. One was in the south and the other in the north, in the delta country.

Finally, in the year 3100 B.C.—that is, 31 centuries before the birth of Christ and the start

26

of our own time—a king named Menes united the two kingdoms. To show that he represented all Egypt, Menes wore two crowns. The narrow red crown was for the delta, and the high white crown was for the south. He lived in a double palace, too, and had two gigantic storehouses for grain.

Menes was still in his teens when he made himself pharaoh. But like all Egyptian rulers, he had enormous power. He was in charge of the army. He served as judge and jury. He decided who should own land. His most important job, however, was the care of the Nile River. It remained the most important responsibility of every pharaoh.

The pharaoh had to see that canals and dams were built. He had to keep them repaired. It was up to him to distribute the river water fairly. When the Nile washed away a boundary, the owner of the field went to the pharaoh about it. The Egyptians expected their pharaoh to know the time and height of the Nile flood so that they could prepare for it.

This woman moves water from the canal to the field by turning a kind of snail-shaped container.

A pharaoh was even supposed to influence the Nile. There is a story about this, carved on the limestone cliffs of the First Cataract. It tells of a time when the Nile rose scarcely at all. Crops failed, and there was a famine. Men stole food as their children wept and clutched their empty stomachs. Their pharaoh, whose name was Zoser, decided to visit Khnum, the god who controlled the Nile. This god was supposed to have made

28

the first man on earth out of mud from the Nile.

When Zoser reached Khnum's temple, he threw himself before a statue of the god and pleaded for his help. The statue replied that Khnum himself had kept the Nile from rising. He was angry because his temple was so shabby. The pharaoh promised to repair it at once. In return, Khnum promised that the Nile would bring good harvests again. And it did.

But the Egyptians did not rely on promises. Every year after that, the pharaoh offered prayers to the Nile. Then he threw it a list of its duties. And to keep on the good side of the river, he dropped into it some gifts.

In times of drought, the soil bakes in the hot sun.

P.I.P. photo by PRESSEHUSET

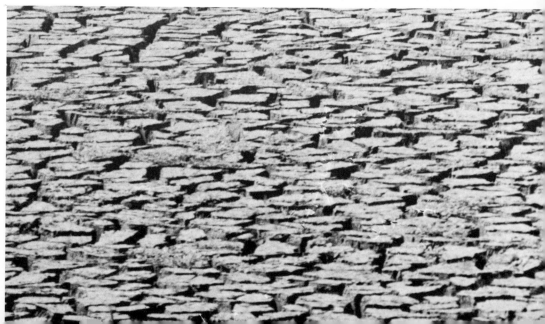

*King Osiris, from
an old Egyptian
wall painting.*
P.I.P. photo

4. The Story of Osiris

The ancient Egyptians had almost 2,000 gods. They worshiped rocks, trees and wells. They bowed before all creation, making gods of bulls, crocodiles, cows, goats, cats, dogs and chickens— anything blessed with life. But of all their gods, two towered over all the rest. One was the sun. The other was the Nile.

The Nile was believed to be a heavenly river on which the sun god crossed the sky in his boat each day. When the Egyptians looked up at the clear soft sky at night, they thought they saw their river stretched across the heavens. Today we call this the Milky Way.

Ancient Egyptians thought the Nile came into Egypt by divine will. They even knew where it entered. It was at the waterfall at the First Cataract near Aswan. Even the rain which fell on other lands was really part of the Nile, they said. One pharaoh said foreigners had to be satisfied with the "Nile from the sky." Only Egypt was blessed with the true Nile.

An Egyptian story told how the sun once grew angry and ran away to the desert, disguised as a lioness. Someone finally persuaded it to return. But before it came back, it stopped to cool off its anger in the Nile cataract.

The religious story that meant most to the Egyptians was about Osiris, the god of the Nile.

It seems that once there were two divine brothers, Set and Osiris. Set was the god of the desert and the burning skies above it. Osiris was the god of the Nile and the earth made fertile by the Nile. He and his wife Isis ruled Egypt so well that they were much loved.

But Set was jealous of his brother and decided to kill him. He had a magnificent chest made exactly the size of Osiris. Then he invited his brother to a banquet and told him the chest would be given to the person who could fit himself inside it. As Set had expected, Osiris tried it. Set promptly slammed the lid shut and threw the chest into the Nile. Osiris drowned, and the current carried the chest away.

While the heartbroken Isis searched for her husband, the wicked Set ruled Egypt. The land dried up, and there were no crops.

At last, Isis found the dead Osiris and buried him. When their young son Horus grew up, however, he fought with Set and banished him. Then Osiris came back to life and reigned as king of heaven, while his son ruled Egypt. Every pharaoh was said to be a son of Horus.

Each year, the story of Osiris was acted out for

*Painting in an ancient tomb
shows Horus leading
the Egyptian queen.*
P.I.P. photo by MIDDLE EAST FEATURES

the Egyptians by the Nile. Just as the god of the Nile died and was reborn, so his river died down and was reborn in the flood. The Egyptians came to believe that they, too, would live again after they died, just as Osiris and the Nile lived and died and lived again, eternally. They even thought Isis helped the rebirth of the Nile. When the Nile first began to rise, people would say, "Isis has shed a tear." Even now, the evening when the Nile starts to rise is sometimes called "the night of the drop" in Egypt.

Ancient circular Egyptian calendar.

Culver Pictures, Inc.

5. Science on the Nile

The early Egyptians were practical as well as superstitious. Although they thought the Nile divine, they worked very hard to control it themselves.

First, they learned to keep track of the river's rise and fall through the year. Wise Egyptians noticed that the Nile usually began to rise the day that Sirius, the Dog Star, rose at dawn. So they made that day the start of their year. (In our calendar this would be July 18.) They found that 365 days must pass before Sirius rose at dawn again. They knew they could expect the Nile to begin its rise that very day.

The Egyptians worked out a 365-day calendar. With some changes, we use the same calendar. No one knows exactly when the Egyptians made their first calendar, but it was thousands of years ago.

Once they had a calendar, the Egyptians divided their year into three seasons of four months each. These were also based on the Nile's changes. The first season was the period of the river's rise, flood and ebb. The second was the planting season. The third was the period of harvest.

Next, the Egyptians wanted to record the exact level of the river during different seasons. They agreed on units of measurement that were always the same, no matter who used them. These were based on one man's measurements, probably those of one particular pharaoh. One of the units of measurement was the length of a man's arm from his elbow to the end of his middle finger. This is about 20 inches as we measure. The Egyptians called this distance a *cubit*.

Actual measurements of the river were made by means of high- and low-water marks placed on prominent buildings or cliffs. These were called *nilometers*. About 20 ancient nilometers still exist today. The most famous, at the island of Elephantine, has marked river levels for 4,500 years. The Nile is the only river that has been studied so long and so carefully.

During the period of the Nile's rise, observers were posted at each nilometer. As the river rose, messengers were sent downstream to report how the present rise compared with those of the past. Rowing with the current, the messengers could outrace the flood. Thus the people had time to prepare for it. And the pharaoh and his ministers knew what kind of crops to expect.

The Greek historian, Herodotus, wrote that the Egyptians prayed for a high-water mark of sixteen ells, or cubits.

"Twelve ells mean hunger," he said, "thirteen,

sufficiency; fourteen, joy; fifteen, security; sixteen, abundance."

There is a famous statue in Rome which shows the Nile as a great bearded god with sixteen little children. The children stand for the sixteen cubits, or ells, of a good Nile flood.

Records kept on stone are permanent, but not particularly convenient. After the Egyptians invented paper and developed writing, it was easier to keep the Nile reports. They made paper out of the papyrus reeds in the Nile marshes, slicing the stems and pressing the strips together.

Papyrus plant from which the Egyptians made paper.

This still readable papyrus was found in the tomb of an Egyptian queen who was buried about 1025 B. C.

(Our word, paper, reminds us that it was first made out of papyrus.) Soot and vegetable gum made good ink. A thin reed served as a pen. Manuscripts written on this Nile reed paper can still be read with ease today, 4,000 years later.

Even with the best controls, the flooding Nile washed away field boundaries. Then the fields had to be measured again. This was not simple. Most fields were very irregular in shape, since every bit of land in the narrow valley had to be put to use. The Egyptians worked out a system of measurement called geometry. The word is made from two Greek words meaning *earth* and *measurement*.

All of this knowledge, plus the engineering they had learned making dams and canals, helped the Egyptians become the greatest builders of the ancient world.

Five thousand years ago, the people of Europe were still living in caves. The Egyptians were building pyramids and sphinxes. They were planting crops, keeping records and inventing mathematics. The main inspiration for all their scientific achievement was the river they thought to be a god.

A Nile River boat in an Egyptian wall painting.

6. Life on the East Bank

In ancient Egypt, every city was really two cities—one for the living and another for the dead. The cities of the living were on the east bank of the Nile. The west bank was reserved for the dead. As a matter of fact, when anyone died, the Egyptians said he "went west."

40

Life on the east bank revolved about the river. The Nile was the only highway the Egyptians ever had. They crossed it as we cross the street. The river went from one end of the narrow kingdom to the other like a great watery turnpike. It made such a satisfactory road that for generations the Egyptians never thought of making wheeled wagons. Instead they used boats for all their transportation. The poor people had skiffs or canoes. The rich had gaily-colored pleasure boats with separate kitchen barges to keep cooking odors at a distance.

Thanks to the Nile, the Egyptians enjoyed treasures from many foreign lands. Their ships were able to sail straight down the river and across the sea. They brought back rare woods, precious stones and gold. Fine craftsmen turned these into beautiful furniture and elaborate jewelry.

Egyptian houses were made of sun-dried bricks of Nile mud and imported wood. Peasant houses were mere huts. The town houses of noblemen and officials were elaborate two- and three-story structures. Country houses were elegant, with flower gardens, fish pools and large airy rooms. Their owners had elaborate banquets. Roast goose or crane fattened on noodles might be on the menu. It was sure to include Nile perch.

The Egyptians enjoyed dancing, storytelling and music. Peasants sang work songs as they planted or irrigated. Large estates had private musicians. Outdoor sports were very popular. Nearly everyone went fishing in the Nile or trapped wild birds in the river marshes. They had cats trained to fetch birds just as dogs do today. More daring hunters went after hippopotamuses and crocodiles.

Egyptian family life seems to have been quite happy. One ancient picture shows giggling children holding on to their father's legs as he tries to snare a fish from the Nile. In another scene a pharaoh jokes with his wife and three little girls as they sail down the river.

Children had many toys and games. Grownups enjoyed games, too, especially a dice game played on a kind of checkerboard. Pets were popular. The Egyptians kept birds, baboons, monkeys and gazelles as well as cats and dogs. When the pets died, they were buried just as people were.

Little is left of the buildings on the east bank today because they were made of perishable materials. One exception is the cluster of stone temples at the ancient towns of Karnak and Luxor.

Karnak and Luxor were joined by an avenue a mile and a half long, lined with stone sphinxes.

An avenue of ram-headed sphinxes join Karnak and Luxor.
P.I.P. photo by MIDDLE EAST FEATURES

Each town was full of temples. Sometimes a pharaoh would build his own temple. Sometimes he added a new part to an old temple.

It took nine pharaohs to build the temple of Amun at Karnak. Ten cathedrals could be put inside its walls. The temple itself is so big that St. Peter's in Rome, the Cathedral at Milan and Nôtre Dame of Paris could fit inside. Each of the twelve main columns in its great hall could hold one hundred men on top. At one time, there were 140 columns in the Karnak temple, adorned with gold, silver, marble or semi-precious stones.

Some years ago the Nile seeped into the temple ruins and loosened its columns. Time rotted others. But even in ruins, the temple of Amun is a marvelous sight.

If we really want to see how well the ancient Egyptians could build, however, we must cross to the west bank of the river.

These giant columns in the temple of Karnak have stood for over 3,000 years.

P.I.P. photo by PRESSEHUSET

The pyramids were among the first of the royal tombs.

7. Mummies, Tombs and Pyramids

To the old Egyptians, the cities on the west bank of the Nile were the most important cities of all. They built their villages of mud brick but they made their tombs of solid rock. They called them their "houses of everlasting." There was a good reason for this.

The Egyptians believed that when they died, their souls actually crossed the Nile and lived on the other side. Tombs were considered homes for

46

the dead, so they were made as cheerful as possible. People who had been rich and happy tried to help their souls go on living exactly as they had in life. They painted pictures of their good times on the walls. They put in their favorite foods, elaborate furniture and precious jewels. Some tombs even had full-sized boats for use on the heavenly Nile.

Sometimes toy-sized models of real objects were put in the tombs. There were many statues, especially little statues of pet animals. Kings and noblemen were buried with hundreds of models of servants who were supposed to do any unpleasant work asked of their masters in heaven. These servants were known as *shawabtys*, or *answerers*. When their noble masters were called to work, the shawabtys were to answer for them: "We are here!"

Since Egyptians believed that the soul remained with a man's body after death, they tried to preserve each body as long as possible. They became expert at the art of embalming, or mummifying, the dead. Each west bank burial area had its own embalmers.

It took 70 days to make a mummy. First, the organs of the body were removed so it was only a shell. The hollow body was soaked in a salt mixture, much as fish is dried today.

Then it was wrapped in yards of linen. Housewives saved old sheets for this purpose. Some of the mummies in museums today are still wrapped in sheets faded from repeated washings. You can still see the laundry marks. It is as if we buried

This old drawing shows embalmers bandaging a mummy while an assistant prepares a coffin. The Bettmann Archive

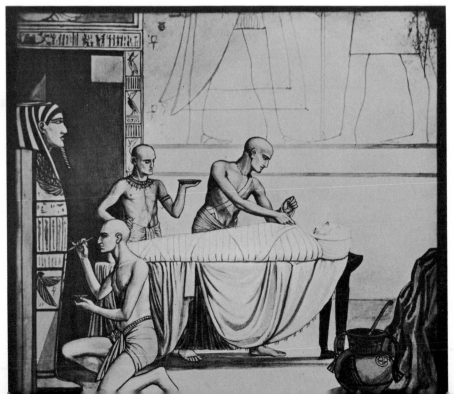

our dead in old camp sheets with name tapes still on them.

A wrapped mummy was placed in a coffin, the more elaborate the better. The coffins of the poor were stacked from floor to ceiling in common graves. Noblemen were buried in tombs called *mastabas*. The kings built themselves tremendous burial structures along the whole length of the Nile.

Among the first of the royal tombs were the pyramids. Most of these were built by the pharaohs of one ruling family who lived from 2680 to 2560 B.C. About 75 of these ancient pyramids remain on the west bank of the Nile. The most famous are the three at Gizeh, near Cairo.

The Great Pyramid at Gizeh is probably the most remarkable structure of all time. Long ago, the Greeks and Romans used to come to see it, just as tourists do today. The Great Pyramid was built as the tomb of a pharaoh named Khufu, or Cheops. It covers thirteen acres, enough space to hold eight football fields. It is as tall as a 40-story skyscraper. It has 2,300,000 blocks of stone, each weighing 2½ tons. If the stones were divided into blocks a foot square, there would be enough blocks to reach two-thirds of the way around the equator. There is enough stone in the Great Pyramid to build a city the size of Topeka, Kansas.

It took 100,000 men working 20 years under the broiling sun to build the Great Pyramid. Just to feed them was a gigantic task. An early historian reported that 1,600 talents of silver (nearly three million dollars in our money) was spent on radishes, onions and garlic alone to feed the laborers. Some of the workers probably were slaves. During the three months of the Nile flood, when farmlands were under water, farmers were expected to work on the pyramids. The pyramid builders had all the manpower they could possibly use—but no machinery.

Nobody knows exactly how the Egyptians managed to build the pyramids without machinery.

Herbert Lanks from Black Star

The Great Pyramid has been a tourist attraction ever since it was built.

But scholars have an idea of how it was done. Probably the great limestone blocks were cut from cliffs on the east side of the Nile. They were floated to the west side when the river was high. Each pyramid was joined to the river bank by a ramp along which the stones were dragged. Oil, water or a mortar of gypsum and sand was put on the slope to make the moving easier.

The 5,000-pound stones were put on sledges. Possibly oxen helped in the backbreaking job.

Finally each stone was fitted into place so tightly that mortar was not needed. Not even the blade of a knife could be slipped between the stones.

To make their measurements, the Egyptians used a knotted string for a ruler. Yet their craftsmanship was so perfect that engineers today say that the 755-foot side of the Great Pyramid is off by less than half an inch.

The second largest pyramid of the Gizeh group was built by a pharaoh named Khafre. Next to it was a mass of natural rock. Khafre had it carved into a lion 66 feet high with his own portrait in stone as its head. Between the paws of the great lion were a temple and altar dedicated to the sun god. This figure beside the Nile is the one we think of as the Great Sphinx. Actually, there were hundreds of other sphinxes built along the Nile.

The mummies of the pharaohs were hidden inside the pyramids. No matter how carefully the graves were concealed, however, robbers found

The Great Sphinx and the Gizeh pyramids.

them. Most of the treasure of the pharaohs is gone, but some of it must still be buried beneath the sands of the Nile Valley. A few years ago, two perfumed funeral barges were found in an underground chamber of the Great Pyramid.

Later pharaohs built different kinds of tombs

to keep their bodies safe. Their capital city was now farther up the Nile at Thebes. Across from Thebes, the Nile is edged by forbidding limestone cliffs. Beyond the cliffs lies an isolated valley. Here, for the next 500 years, generations of kings put their tombs. It came to be known as the "Valley of the Tombs of Kings." There were probably more precious stones, gold, paintings and sculpture in this valley at one time than in any other spot in the world. The last king was buried in the valley over 3,000 years ago.

These pharaohs also built the temples which remain on the west bank of the Nile to this day. The massive structures seem to boast of the power of the pharaohs who had ordered them built. One pharaoh put two red stone statues of himself outside of his temple. Each was 65 feet high and weighed 700 tons. One of the statues was jarred in an earthquake. Afterward, when the first rays of the sun warmed it, it made a musical sound. This "Singing Colossus" was a favorite tourist attraction during the days of the Roman Empire.

The Colossi of Memnon.
Ewing Galloway

One temple in Thebes is unlike all the others. It was built by a queen named Hatshepsut. Hatshepsut's temple has gracious terraces sloping toward the Nile. Its beautiful gardens once were filled with strange, perfumed foreign trees. Its rose-colored stones are still lovely. Hatshepsut tried to be as kingly as possible. She even had herself portrayed wearing a beard. But she had many enemies, especially her younger brother who wanted the throne for himself. Finally he had her killed. Then he tried to destroy every trace of her. He had her statues heated with fire and chilled with cold water to make them burst. But the statues have been rebuilt, and the beautiful temple still stands, reminding everyone of the great queen.

As it turned out, the pharaohs buried in the Valley of the Tombs of Kings were no safer than their pyramid-building ancestors. Their graves were robbed, too. So far as we know, only one royal mummy was untouched. That was the mummy of Tutankhamen. He is called the Golden

The temple of
Queen Hatshepsut.
P.I.P. photo by
MIDDLE EAST FEATURES

Pharaoh because his mummy was still in its casket of gold when his tomb was discovered in 1922. Tutankhamen became pharaoh between the ages of nine and twelve and died before he was eighteen. He was still so much of a child that his favorite slingshot was buried with him.

As a king, he was quite unimportant. But to us he is important because his is the only Nile tomb that has been found unharmed in recent times. Looking at the gold inlaid chariots, the gilt couches, the caskets of jewels and rich robes buried with Tutankhamen, we have a good idea of how other pharaohs were buried.

It is possible that even richer tombs lie beneath the sandy cliffs on the west bank of the Nile.

Tutankhamen's golden mask which covered the face of his mummy.

8. The Riddle
of the Rosetta Stone

The ancient kingdom of Egypt lasted for nearly 35 centuries, longer than any civilization in history. Then enemies overcame it. Nearly two thousand years ago, the glamorous Egyptian queen, Cleopatra, tried to restore her country's power. She even offered to marry her Roman conquerors. But Egypt fell, and Cleopatra killed herself by letting a poisonous snake bite her.

Eventually, Egypt disappeared from history. She became an Arab colony. Her great cities fell into ruins; her monuments were covered by sand. The dams and canals along the Nile fell into disrepair. The once proud Nile Valley was a collection of mud-hut villages.

By the time of the Middle Ages, no one knew that the great Nile civilization had ever existed. The pyramids still stood, but it was a mystery who had built them or why.

Then, in 1798, the French commander Napoleon led an army into Egypt. He was not interested in ancient history, but in Egyptian ports. He wanted control of the Mediterranean Sea.

Still Napoleon took a few scholars along with him to the unknown country. What they saw as they traveled up the Nile made them gasp. They had so much to write about that it took them fifteen years to get it all down on paper. Even then, they were unable to read the inscriptions on the thousands of monuments, scrolls and statues they found. The written Egyptian language had been forgotten, too.

Ancient Egyptian hieroglyphics.

The Rosetta Stone.

P.I.P. photo

There was one clue to the mysterious inscriptions, however. In 1799, an officer in Napoleon's army found an intriguing stone near Rosetta at the west mouth of the Nile. It was a slab of black basalt, measuring three feet nine inches by two feet four inches. It was divided into three panels covered with different kinds of writing. The top panel had hieroglyphics, the ancient Egyptian picture writing. The middle was in a cursive form of Egyptian hieroglyphics which was used for rapid writing. The bottom panel was in Greek which scholars could read. The stone was called the Rosetta Stone, after the spot where it was found.

Many scholars studied the inscriptions. They had an idea that the three panels said the same thing. If they could match the Greek inscription to the Egyptian hieroglyphics, they would have some idea of the lost language. The mystery was finally solved by a young French language student named Jean François Champollion.

Champollion studied the stone day and night. He made out enough of the Egyptian writing to know that some signs could be matched to Greek letters. Then he managed to put some of the letters opposite some of the Egyptian signs. Eventually, he could read the whole inscription. Today, it is possible to decipher almost every inscription left in the Nile Valley.

It took 23 years for the Rosetta Stone to be deciphered. It had taken Napoleon only 23 days to conquer Egypt. But Napoleon's victory was brief. Champollion's victory helped scholars read the whole record of ancient Egypt. It was the key that opened a lost world.

Cairo, the largest modern city on the Nile.

Egyptian State Tourist Administration

9. Solving a Mystery

Just about the time that ancient Egypt was being rediscovered, explorers began to work on another Nile mystery. This mystery was the source of the great African river.

The Nile was one of the first rivers known to man, but its origin was one of the world's great puzzles. The Egyptians never tried to solve the puzzle. It was enough for them that the Nile came from heaven.

Over the years, travelers turned up with strange tales of a Nile beyond the borders of Egypt. Some said there were curious animals on its shores. Others reported seeing cannibals and dwarfs. There were even wild stories that the Nile came from mountains covered with snow right at the equator. After the Romans conquered Egypt, the Emperor Nero sent an expedition to find out what lay beyond the First Cataract. His soldiers never got past the sudd.

A hundred years later, in 150 A.D., the Greek geographer, Ptolemy, drew a map that included the Nile. He showed it rising from two lakes between two snow-capped mountains. Ptolemy called them the *Lunae Montes*, or Mountains of the Moon. Oddly enough, that is exactly what the native Africans called the mountains.

How Ptolemy got his information about the Nile is another mystery. So far as we know, only one outsider ever got to a source of the river before the late eighteenth and nineteenth centuries. The Nile Valley was covered with ruins, but beyond Egypt there was only wilderness. The interior of Africa was as remote as outer space. Actually, we probably know more about outer space today than anyone knew about the heart of Africa then.

There were no maps and no roads. Streams were often impassable. The wild steamy countryside was covered with thick jungles and dangerous swamps. Where the Nile was not choked with reeds, it might be plunging down a precipice. The water was full of crocodiles, and fierce animals drank and bathed at its shore. Poisonous snakes coiled in the underbrush. Tropical storms broke unexpectedly.

There were only a few native villages, and no one could tell whether their inhabitants would be

A crocodile suns himself on the banks of the Nile.

East Africa Tourist Travel Association

friendly or not. A traveler from the outside had to be prepared to fight his way on foot through the torrid jungles, carrying all his supplies with him. He faced malaria and other tropical diseases. It took two Portuguese explorers nine years to cross Africa during this period.

Portuguese priests had been in Ethiopia off and on since the seventeenth century. One of these, Father Pedro Paez, reported that an Ethiopian king had actually taken him to the source of the Blue Nile.

In 1770, James Bruce, an Englishman, explored the Blue Nile. Forgetting Father Paez, he announced that he had discovered its source. He wrote, "I stood in rapture." He followed the river all the way to Khartoum. He could not make the entire journey by water, though. Even today the river is so wild in places that it would wreck a steel boat. Bruce was not even able to travel along the shore, because the Blue Nile lies in a canyon for much of its way to the Sudan.

When he got back to England, Bruce wrote a

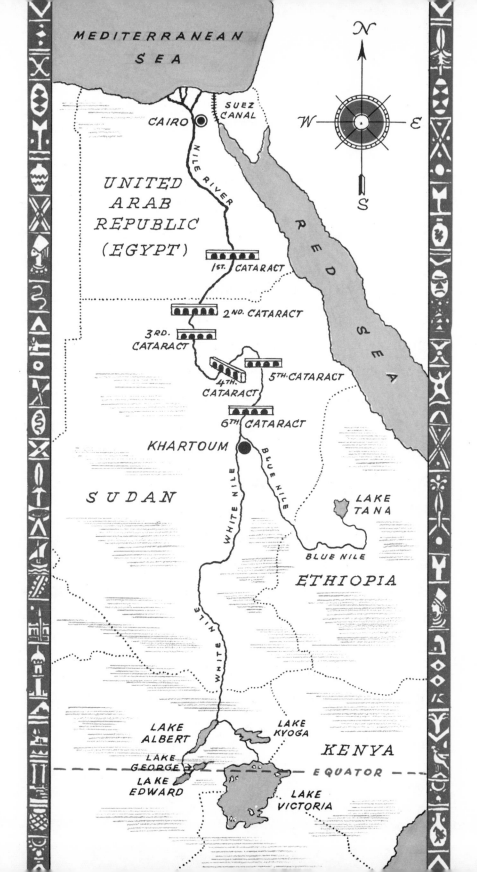

long book about how he had solved the mystery of the Nile. Of course, he was not even half right. He had discovered—or rather, rediscovered—one source of the river, but it was not the only source. It was not even the main source. That still lay undiscovered in central Africa, a thousand miles from Bruce's Ethiopian spring.

Another generation passed before a new attempt was made to find the true source of the Nile. Then, in 1856, two more Englishmen joined forces to make the river disclose its secret. They were Richard Francis Burton and John Hanning Speke.

Burton spoke 29 languages and claimed to understand the jabbering of monkeys as well. He had once lived with a colony of 30 monkeys in order to learn their speech. When he was older, he translated the stories of the Arabian Nights into English. If you ever enjoyed "Sinbad the Sailor" or "Ali Baba and the Forty Thieves," you can thank Richard Francis Burton.

Speke was a quiet, almost shy man. He loved

John Hanning Speke.

animals and collected rare birds. His great ambition was to have a natural history museum of his own in England.

The two men started their journey across Africa from Bagamoyo, a town on the Indian Ocean, instead of going up the Nile from Egypt. They wanted to avoid the swamps that had stopped the Romans. Speke set out first—on foot. Burton left two days later, grandly perched on a camel. He soon caught up with Speke.

Where possible, the two explorers followed jungle trails from village to village. Often, they had to hack their path through the dense vegetation. Their expedition had supplies for two years. There were 170 people in the party, including wives and children of the porters who carried all the supplies on their heads.

The caravan must have been a startling sight. First came guides, wearing elaborate headdresses. Behind them were the drummers. Next came porters with beads and cloth to be used for trading. Then came porters with such equipment as food, tents, guns, medicines, blankets, pots, books, ink, instruments, cigars, snuff, fishhooks, brandy, rugs and umbrellas. Like true Englishmen, Speke and Burton took two umbrellas apiece with them into the depths of Africa. After the porters came the women and children leading the cattle which were to help feed the party. Bringing up the rear was the expedition's armed guard.

The caravan generally started before dawn each day. It was too hot for them to travel after eight o'clock in the morning. Sometimes the party had to stay in one place for days while Burton and Speke negotiated with a local chief for permission to go through his territory. Each chief had to be given presents.

At every stop, the porters set up a new camp. Sometimes they hunted for meat or bought grain in a nearby village. Burton mentioned in his diary that the porters often danced in the moonlight after dinner was over. The natives used to stand near the camp and peer at the strange Englishmen, the first white men they had ever seen.

It was a hard journey. Animals became sick and died. Many porters ran away. Those who remained were weak with disease. The caravan was swamped by water from cloudbursts.

Finally, the expedition arrived at what is now Lake Tanganyika. Speke and Burton were very excited. But they could find no trace of any river flowing north. Lake Tanganyika could not be the source of the Nile. By this time Burton had a

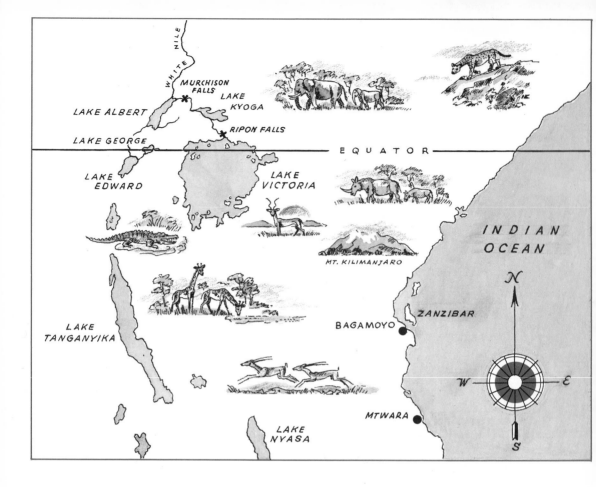

badly diseased jaw, so the expedition went back to a nearby village. Here the two men were told of another lake much bigger than Lake Tanganyika. The natives called it *Nyanza*, which means *great water*. It was just three weeks' walk away. Speke was half blind, but he decided to go on alone and investigate the new lake.

On August 3, 1858, nearly two years after the

start of the expedition, Speke came to a broad blue lake with beaches of yellow sand. It had lovely shade trees and thick papyrus marshes filled with storks and ibises. Along the shore were native villages.

Later Speke said the lake was "so broad you could not see across it, and so long that nobody knew its length." We know its size today. It is exactly twice as big as the entire country of Belgium. Speke was sure that the lake was the source of the Nile, but he knew he had to do more exploring to prove it. So he named the lake Victoria Nyanza in honor of his queen, Victoria, and rejoined Burton.

By this time, the expedition had pushed 1,500 miles through the jungle, just about half the

The sacred ibis of Egypt.

distance across the United States. The caravan had another four months' journey back to Bagamoyo and the Indian Ocean.

Speke could not convince Burton that Victoria Nyanza was the source of the Nile. Burton still thought the source was near Lake Tanganyika. So the two explorers parted and Speke returned to England to raise money for a new expedition.

The Nile at Aswan. Egyptian State Tourist Administration

10. Up Where the Nile Begins

Two years later, John Speke was back at Lake Victoria with a new partner, J. L. Grant. There were three kingdoms around the lake, Bunyoro, Buganda and Karagwe. Except for Arab traders, no strangers had ever visited them before. Speke had to travel through all three kingdoms to explore the entire lake shore.

Bunyoro was a harsh, dry country, with a king, Kamrasi, who liked to be given presents. He kept Speke and Grant waiting in his palace until he thought he had gotten every possible gift out of them. Then he gave them permission to proceed across his kingdom to Karagwe.

Karagwe was full of wild animals—elephants, antelope, rhinoceroses and hippopotamuses. The king of Karagwe, Rumanika, was not as greedy as Kamrasi, but he had a strange sense of humor. He told Speke that his donkeys would not be allowed into Buganda, the last of the Lake Victoria kingdoms, unless he put trousers on them. Then he allowed the party to continue to Buganda, a six weeks' walk away.

Mutesa, the ruler of Buganda, was a cruel and dangerous youth. When Mutesa walked, he strutted like a lion. His subjects were supposed to throw themselves to the ground whenever he finished talking. If anyone offended him, he had the culprit executed on the spot. Even with a ruler of this type, Mutesa's kingdom was the most attractive of the three. Its fields were fertile, and its houses were neat and surrounded by gardens.

Speke decided to be as regal as Mutesa. He put on his best suit when he arrived and dressed his men in red blankets. Impressed, Mutesa accepted Speke's gifts graciously. He even gave some gifts

Ripon Falls, outlet of Africa's largest lake, Lake Victoria.

in return, among them a rat and a porcupine. Then he allowed Speke to walk on.

Finally, six long years after Speke and Burton first thought of looking for the source of the Nile, Speke reached the outlet of Lake Victoria. Here the lake poured over a waterfall into a stream

77

which flowed clearly and surely to the north. Thousands of fish jumped out of the falls. Below, sleeping peacefully on the rocks, lay hippopotamuses and crocodiles. There was no question in Speke's mind. He had found the source of the Nile. Full of joy, he stared at the water.

"It was a sight that attracted one for hours," he noted in his journal.

He also wrote, "I say that old Father Nile without any doubt rises in the Victoria Nyanza."

Speke called his discovery Ripon Falls, naming it after the Englishman who had helped finance his second Nile expedition.

On his way back, Speke made the mistake of stopping at Bunyoro again. King Kamrasi took the only possible gift Speke had left, his gold chronometer.

Speke had done all his exploring on foot. He never so much as rode a donkey from the time he left Bagamoyo to the time he returned.

Years later, a granite block marked the spot

where Speke had watched the fish leaping at the falls. On it was a plaque saying:

SPEKE

DISCOVERED THIS

SOURCE OF THE

NILE

ON THE 28 JULY 1862.

In the 1950's, a hydroelectric dam was put up at Ripon Falls. Today the place where the plaque stood is deep under water.

A year or so after Speke discovered Ripon Falls, another Englishman, Sir Samuel Baker, and his beautiful young wife followed the Nile to its source. They started from Khartoum. Their lavishly-equipped expedition even included pet monkeys and birds. It took them two years just to get through the sudd swamps. But they did get through. Romans might give up. Not the Bakers.

Farther ahead, natives attacked them with poisoned arrows. Wild animals wandered into their tents. At times the Bakers had no food and had to eat grass. Mrs. Baker had brain fever and malaria. But as her husband says in his book about their journey, "She was not a screamer!"

Finally, the Bakers got to Bunyoro. Sir Samuel followed Speke's example and put on his best suit. Mrs. Baker caused a sensation by washing her long yellow hair in a stream. Nobody had ever seen hair like that in Bunyoro. But when Kamrasi received the Bakers, he was interested only in their presents. He accepted guns, beads and rugs gratefully, and then asked Sir Samuel to do him a favor. Would he be good enough to fix the chronometer Speke had given him? It seems Kamrasi had taken it apart to see what made it tick and could not put it together again. Unfortunately, Sir Samuel couldn't either.

Eventually the Bakers pushed on. They discovered another vast lake which they called Lake Albert, in honor of Queen Victoria's husband. Nearby was a waterfall even bigger than the one Speke had discovered. The Bakers named theirs after the Englishman who had helped them

Murchison Falls is the Nile's largest waterfall.

finance their expedition. His name was Murchison. As they were admiring their mighty waterfall, the Bakers were charged by a hippopotamus, but they got away unharmed. Murchison Falls is now part of a huge national park for wild animals, hippopotamuses included.

After the Bakers, other explorers finished mapping the sources of the Nile. One of these was a newspaperman working for an American paper, Henry M. Stanley of *The New York Herald*.

In 1899, the British hacked the first real channel through the sudd swamps. They put in a system of railroads and steamers which now made it possible to go the whole length of the Nile. For the first time in its history, the Nile was open from central Africa to the Mediterranean.

There are still parts of the Blue Nile which are unexplored, however. In the 1920's, a British major, R. E. Cheesman, became the first white man to go all around Lake Tana. But even he could not travel the length of the Blue Nile.

In World War II, the British Army followed the Nile upstream some distance into Ethiopia, but it could not go all the way. A few years ago, American engineers began a study of the gorge of the Blue Nile. Alan Moorehead, doing research for his fine book about the river, traveled in a helicopter with these engineers. The helicopter dipped in and out of the gorge. He wrote, "The air was thick and hot, and one felt the curious stillness and completeness that rests on places that have never been disturbed by man."

Even today the floor of the Blue Nile gorge has still never been "disturbed by man."

Modern Cairo.   Egyptian State Tourist Administration

11. The High Dam of Aswan

An ancient Egyptian would be quite at home in many Egyptian villages today. Goats still walk on the roofs of the mud-brick houses. Fields are still watered by the river. Small boats do most of the carting. And villagers still think that drinking Nile water keeps them strong even though well water is really much safer.

Modern Egypt covers nearly 400,000 square miles. But most of her population still lives on the banks of the Nile and in the delta at its mouth. This is an area of less than 14,000 square miles. The Nile Valley is still the only land in

Egypt that is not desert. It is as if the entire Atlantic Coast of the United States were barren except for the small state of Maryland. With no more rain than in ancient times, Egypt still depends on the Nile for all of its water. And because modern countries require electricity, it looks to the Nile for water power as well.

In one respect, an ancient Egyptian would find life more crowded than it was thousands of years ago. Only seven million people lived in the Nile Valley in his day. Now the long narrow strip must feed a population of 26 million. In some

Grass-roofed huts are crowded together in this Nile village.

P.I.P. photo by MIDDLE EAST FEATURES

*In many places along the Nile plowing is done with a wooden plow
just as it was a thousand years ago.*

places 1,500 people live on one square mile of
land. Even though the valley has some of the
most fertile soil in the world, many go hungry.

But modern Egyptians have as much faith in
the Nile as their ancestors did. They, too, are
turning to the river for help. They are building
a new dam which will make use of every drop
of the Nile's water. The dam will help them turn

deserts into farmland. It will double the amount of electricity available for Egyptian industry.

The Aswan High Dam is the biggest project in the Nile's long history. When it is finished, it will complete the harnessing of the river begun so many thousands of years ago. Beside it, even the pyramids will look small. The bulk of the dam will be sixteen times that of the Great Pyramid, mightiest work of any pharaoh. No one knows how much the dam will cost before it is finished, but it will be at least a billion dollars.

In the days of the pharaohs, slaves and free men worked under the broiling sun. Many died of the heat. They had no machinery. Men's backs and muscles did all the work, with only ropes and oiled ramps to help them. Today the 18,000 men on the job at Aswan have machines to help them. Most of the work is done at night, too, because day temperatures at the dam site sometimes go as high as 140 degrees. Unlike the workers of old Egypt, today's workers need not depend on daylight. The construction site is floodlighted.

The High Dam will replace the old Aswan Dam, one of the first large dams ever built. The present dam forms a lake 200 miles long. This can release 1,500 tons of water every second for irrigation during times of drought. Other smaller dams along the Nile's course furnish water for irrigation, too. They make it possible for some fields to yield two to three crops a year. Irrigated fields, however, must be fertilized, since the river silt drops to the bottom of the storage lakes instead of renewing the fields.

The High Dam will form a reservoir 367 miles long. It will be the largest man-made lake in the world. The new lake will hold enough water to turn another million more acres of desert into fertile land. It will make it possible to irrigate 700,000 more acres in Upper Egypt now watered only once a year by the Nile flood. This extra farmland will mean an end to hunger for millions of Egyptians. At present, Egypt has only six million acres to feed her people. With a population less than seven times that of Egypt's,

Model of the High Dam at Aswan.   Egyptian State Tourist Administration

the United States has two hundred times as much farmland.

The electricity generated at the High Dam will help fight hunger, too. It will give more than power for industry. It will help Egypt modernize her farms.

But the High Dam will mean a sacrifice for Egypt. A dam works by holding back the water of a river and storing it until it is needed. The

The Temple of Isis, left, on the island of Philae.

land over which the water backs up is covered. The High Dam will make the Nile back up over almost all of Nubia. The whole area will be part of the High Dam lake. Hundreds of monuments, including the great temple at Abu Simbel, will also be under water.

Abu Simbel is one of the wonders of the world. Over 3,000 years ago, a powerful pharaoh named Ramses had it carved out of the red sandstone cliffs of Nubia. The Nile was a great help to the royal artisans, for they cut the rock as they wished and let the debris fall into the river. Inside the temple they placed an altar so artfully

90

that on the first day of spring and the first day of autumn the first rays of the sun touched it.

Outside, four gigantic statues of Ramses were carved into the cliff. Three of the 67-foot-high figures still gaze across the Nile into the rising sun. The top of the fourth fell to the ground many centuries ago.

Another monument threatened by the High Dam is Philae, an island in the Nile. Philae was a center for the worship of Isis. The temple built

The island of Philae as it looks when flooded.

in her honor is the main attraction of the island's many buildings.

Philae is located between the present low Aswan Dam and the site of the new High Dam. Since the turn of the century, when the low dam was built, Philae has been flooded nine months of every year. When the High Dam is complete, the flooding will not be so great, but the water will rise and fall more often. The stones of the temples will begin to wear down more rapidly.

In 1960, UNESCO, the scientific and cultural body of the United Nations, began to raise money to save the monuments. It has become the largest fund-raising campaign for archaeology in history. Nearly $87,000,000 will be needed to save just the special few. Many nations have pledged their help. Our own country has contributed $4,000,000.

Scholars from all over the world have come to Nubia to help move temples and statues to safety. The Egyptian government is giving some of these to the various countries in return for their help.

In the summer of 1963, a group of Swedish

Four enormous statues guard the Temple of Abu Simbel.

engineers suggested a way to save the temples of Abu Simbel. Their plan calls for cutting the temples into blocks and moving them to the top of the hill in which they are embedded. Experts say the project will take five years and cost $40,000,000.

The Egyptian government and the UNESCO committee have approved the plan, and over forty nations have pledged the money that will be needed.

The protection of Philae will not be as difficult or as expensive. Engineers have suggested circling the island with a low dike. The island would stay dry the year around and would be an attraction to tourists.

Some people think it is wrong to spend so much on ancient monuments. They think the world should let the Nile have the buildings and use the money for better purposes.

The question is still not settled. Meanwhile, the High Dam nearby grows taller. Each day, the quarries that furnished stone for the pyramids produce more stone for Aswan. But the stones are building something better than monuments. They are helping the great Nile make a better life for the people of Egypt today.

Index

Meet the Author

VIOLET WEINGARTEN was born in San Francisco and grew up in New York City, two cities separated by a distance just about as long as the Nile River. After her graduation from Cornell University, she worked as a newspaper reporter. Her assignments included everything from royal visits and murder trials to bagpipe-playing contests. Now she works with her husband, Victor, in their public relations office. She has written scripts for several prize-winning motion pictures produced by Mr. Weingarten.

A few years ago, the Weingartens and their two daughters, Jan and Kathy, took a long European trip. They traveled by plane, ship, train, bus, car, gondola, cogtrain, subway, trolley, helicopter and donkey. Of all the places they visited, they loved the ancient ruins on the islands of Greece the best. When they came home, Mrs. Weingarten and Kathy, then 13, wrote a book about their travels.

The Weingartens' home is deep in woods outside Mount Kisco, New York, and was originally built by the writer, Theodore Dreiser.

It is enhanced by a beagle dog and two fat orange cats.